D0194858

A GIFT FOR:

★ ★ ★ ★ ★ ★ ★ ★

FROM:

★ ★ ★ ★ ★ ★ ★ ★

★ ★ ★ ★ ★ ★ ★ ★ ★ ★

THE WIT & WISDOM OF OUR
TROOPS

★ ★ ★ ★ ★ ★ ★ ★ ★ ★

AN INSPIRING COLLECTION OF QUOTES
HONORING OUR COURAGEOUS
MILITARY MEN AND WOMEN

★ **MATTHEW ELIOT** ★

Hallmark

CIDER MILL
PRESS

BOOK
PUBLISHERS

Kennebunkport, Maine

★ CONTENTS ★

INTRODUCTION

America's origin, its unprecedented levels of freedom and opportunity, and the unsurpassed quality of life its citizens enjoy are inextricably linked to the efforts of those who have served in its Armed Forces. Even a cursory glance at its history proves that the backbone of the American experiment consists of the valor, sacrifice, and strength of those who fought to gain and keep her.

While the grit, courage, and conviction of these troops are widely acknowledged and appreciated, the considerable quality of the minds contained within their ranks is often overlooked. Their impressive feats of body and spirit tend to drown out the products of their intellect. And yet it is clear that our troops not only possess a profound intelligence but also a unique perspective on the world and human nature.

Consider the quick thinking necessary to thrive in a situation where everyone you know would likely freeze. Consider the poise and strategic gifts required to stay calm under fire and ensure your own safety and that of the people under your command. Consider the insights that would result from being tossed into such trials. Consider the maturity and wisdom someone would need in order to have the soldier's viewpoint, to recognize that serving something larger than yourself is what gives life value.

We picture a solider standing in a crisp uniform with impeccable posture, mouth set firm. Our vision is invariably of someone who is silent and stoic, someone who retains this posture no matter the situation. While there is some truth in this image, particularly in their ability to remain cool under fire, this image can rob them of their voice and deny them the ability to articulate the unique perspective their experience and service has provided. This book is a small step toward correcting this oversight and advancing a claim that a soldier's vision extends far beyond that which is in the sights of their weapon—that their greatest asset is, in fact, their mind.

As we work through the words of those who have gone on to become President of the United States, those who have been honored as Nobel laureates, and those whose exemplary work has earned them the Congressional Medal of Honor, we can see that it is their brilliance and mental acuity that produces the combination of courage, belief, and discipline that leaves so many in awe.

They are the backbone of this country, and have been since its creation. These individuals are not just a part of our history, they are a part of our families and part of our communities. In their stories we learn about ourselves, our past, and where we are headed. Their words teach us about the depth of the American spirit, remind us of the sacrifice required to maintain it, and encourage us to believe that the extraordinary discipline, courage, belief, and humility we commonly attribute to them are also qualities that we possess. These are qualities we can access if we pay attention and hold ourselves to the ideals they do, if we listen to what it is they are saying.

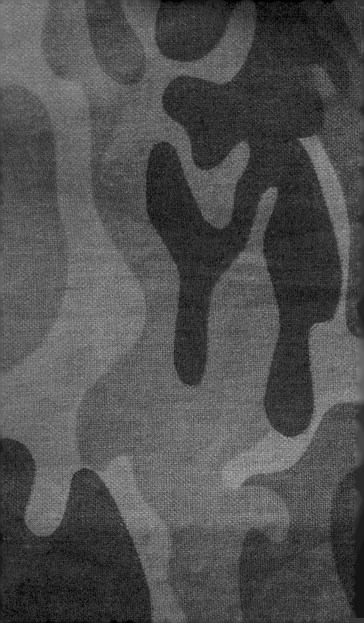

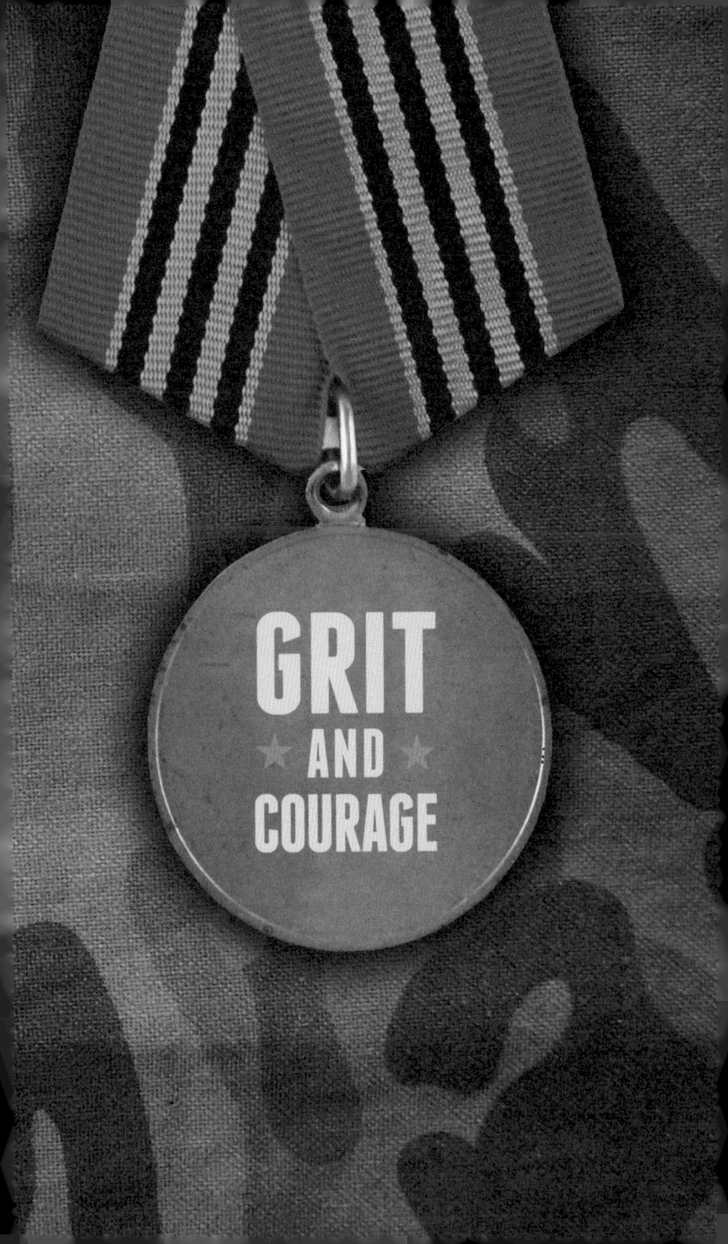
GRIT
AND
COURAGE

"War is fear cloaked in courage."

GEN. WILLIAM WESTMORELAND

"Bravery is being the only one
who knows you're afraid."

COL. DAVID HACKWORTH

★ ★ ★ ★ ★ ★ ★ ★

Exceptional Bravery

As a member of a combined SEAL and Iraqi Army Sniper Overwatch Element, tasked with providing early warning and stand-off protection from a rooftop in an insurgent-held sector of Ar Ramadi, Iraq, Petty Officer Michael A. Monsoor distinguished himself by his exceptional bravery in the face of grave danger.

In the early morning, insurgents prepared to execute a coordinated attack by reconnoitering the area around the element's position. Element snipers thwarted the enemy's initial attempt by eliminating two insurgents. The enemy continued to assault the element, engaging them with a rocket-propelled grenade and small arms fire. As enemy activity increased, Petty Officer Monsoor took position with his machine gun between two teammates on an outcropping of the roof. While the SEALs vigilantly watched for enemy activity, an insurgent threw a hand grenade from an unseen location, which bounced off Monsoor's chest and landed in front of him.

Even though he could have escaped the blast, Monsoor chose instead to protect his teammates. Instantly and without regard for his own safety, he threw himself onto the grenade to absorb the force of the explosion with his body, saving the lives of his two teammates. By his undaunted courage, fighting spirit, and unwavering devotion to duty in the face of certain death, Petty Officer Monsoor gallantly gave his life for his country, thereby reflecting great credit upon himself and upholding the highest traditions of the U.S. Naval Service.

"What makes this country so special
is not our accomplishments;
it's how we bounce back from adversity,
it's how we beat back our fears, it's the way
we soldier through disappointment and trial.
These are the hallmarks of a great people."

ADMIRAL MICHAEL MULLEN

. . . .

"An American soldier will fight harder,
live on less food, and accept more
hardships than any other soldier
on the face of the globe."

GEN. JOHN PERSHING

. . . .

"The troops were hardy, being inured to fatigue,
and they appeared in their respective camps as ready
and fit for duty as they had ever been in their lives.
I doubt whether an equal body of men of any nation,
take them man for man, officer for officer,
was ever gotten together that would have proved
their equal in a great battle."

ULYSSES S. GRANT

"It would seem that every war our nation has fought
was supposed to be over in a few short weeks or months.
That is simply not the nature of war.
Wars are complex, and while battles may be won
in short order, it takes years to address the
underlying political, social, and cultural issues
that lead to conflict in the first place."

MAJ. GEN. WAYNE W. GRIGSBY JR.

"What a cruel thing war is…
to fill our hearts with hatred
instead of love for our neighbors."

CONFEDERATE GENERAL ROBERT E. LEE

"Courage is fear holding on
a minute longer."

GEN. GEORGE S. PATTON

"Physical fear is always part of the battlefield.
We've overcome physical fear
by developing new instincts."

GEN. MARTIN DEMPSEY

"Master your trade and never, never, never quit!
Enough motivation, persistence, and willpower
will get you through everything."

1ST SGT. SANDREA CRUZ

★ ★ ★ ★ ★ ★ ★ ★ ★

"Onward we stagger, and if the tanks come,
may God help the tanks."

COL. WILLIAM O. DARBY

. . . .

"I wish to have no connection with
any ship that does not sail fast; for
I intend to go in harm's way."

JOHN PAUL JONES

. . . .

"It is not enough to fight. It is the spirit which
we bring to the fight that decides the issue.
It is morale that wins the victory."

GEN. GEORGE C. MARSHALL

"Our cause must never be abandoned; it is the cause
of free institutions and self-government."

GEN. GEORGE McCLELLAN

"What really counts is not the immediate act of courage or of valor, but those who bear the struggle day in and day out—not the sunshine patriots but those who are willing to stand for a long period of time."

JOHN F. KENNEDY

. . . .

"Their sacrifices drive us to persevere. They drive us to finish this noble mission well. And they drive us to win."

GEN. JOHN CAMPBELL

. . . .

"We have sent men and women from the Armed Forces of the United States to other parts of the world throughout the past century to put down oppression. We defeated Fascism. We defeated Communism. We saved Europe in World War I and World War II. We were willing to do it, glad to do it. We went to Korea. We went to Vietnam. All in the interest of preserving the rights of people."

COLIN POWELL

"A pint of sweat will save a gallon of blood."

GEN. GEORGE PATTON

"I promise that my son will grow up appreciating the sacrifices of men he never knew."

STAFF SERGEANT RYAN PITTS

"Brave rifles! Veterans!
You have been baptized in fire
and blood and have come out steel!"

LIEUT. GEN. WINFIELD SCOTT

"To all who mourn a son, a brother, a husband, a father, a friend—I can only offer you the gratitude of a nation, for your loved one served his country with distinction and honor."

GEORGE H.W. BUSH

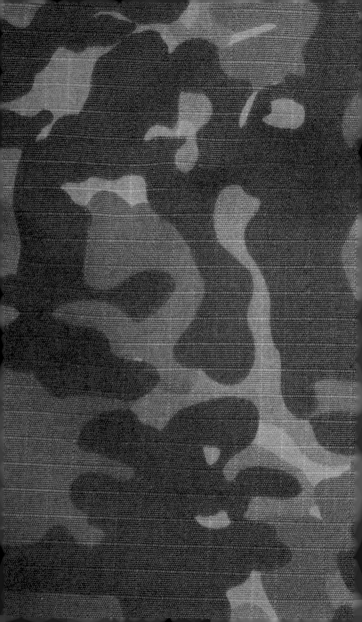

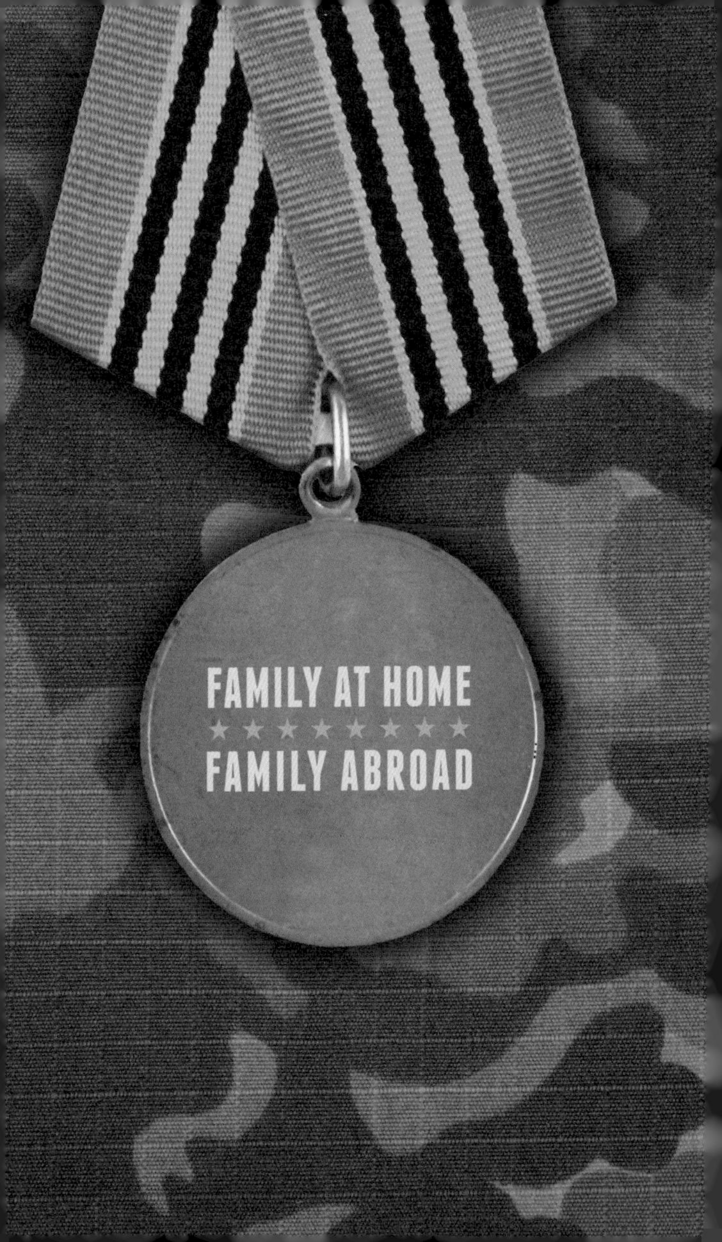
FAMILY AT HOME
FAMILY ABROAD

★ ★ ★ ★ ★ ★ ★ ★ ★

"The currency of our profession
is a bond of trust and a deep sense
of caring about each other.
The nature of our business demands
that we rise above the fear and doubt."

GEN. ROBERT CONE

No Man Alone

"Major [Bruce] Crandall's unit was transporting a battalion of soldiers to a remote spot in the Ia Drang Valley, to a landing zone called X-Ray. After several routine lifts into the area, the men on the ground came under a massive attack from the North Vietnamese army. On Major Crandall's next flight, three soldiers on his helicopter were killed, three more were wounded. But instead of lifting off to safety, Major Crandall kept his chopper on the ground—in the direct line of enemy fire—so that four wounded soldiers could be loaded aboard.

Major Crandall flew the men back to base, where the injuries could be treated. At that point, he had fulfilled his mission. But he knew that soldiers on the ground were outnumbered and low on ammunition. So Major Crandall decided to fly back into X-Ray. He asked for a volunteer to join him. Captain Ed Freeman stepped forward. In their unarmed choppers, they flew through a cloud of smoke and a wave of bullets. They delivered desperately needed supplies.

If Major Crandall had stopped here he would have been a hero. But he didn't stop. … Fourteen times he flew into what they called the Valley of Death. … When they touched down on their last flight, Major Crandall and Captain Freeman had spent more than fourteen hours in the air. They had evacuated some seventy wounded men."

George W. Bush

"The young men who succeed in Navy SEAL training are the young men who have parents who had high expectations of them. They were not surprised to see the young men succeed in these programs, because they had programmed them to finish what they start, to do their best—they have high expectations. If any one trait runs through all these people, it's good parenting."

DICK COUCH

"All of the strategic planning, all of the transformation I just spoke about is impossible without the single, greatest asset we have … our people."

SECRETARY GORDON R. ENGLAND

"You must ask yourself, 'How did these men do it?'
Or, 'What compelled them to take these actions?'
Again we return to our dedication to our brothers.
We were a family whose bonds were forged
in the fires of combat. Our brothers' lives
were more important than our own.
If they were in a fight, then we wanted to be there.
They would never stand alone."

STAFF SERGEANT RYAN PITTS

"I can make men follow me to hell."

OFFICER PHILIP KEARNY

"The nature of war is immutable:
You need trust and connection."

MAJ. GEN. JAMES MATTIS

"We need to make sure that we have one another's back and recognize the fact that patriots come in all different sizes, shapes, colors. Not all of them wear uniforms, some of them are employers, some of them are the family members who stay at home and take care of business."

LT. GENERAL HARRY M. WYATT

"I also want to express my gratitude to your families at home. I know firsthand the sacrifices they make every day to support us while we're deployed. In many ways, these separations are harder on them than on us. Please convey to them how important your mission remains here; and how vital their support is to our success."

GEN. JOHN CAMPBELL

"When a month or two goes by, fifteen minutes [on the phone] is like a second."

JENNIFER MUELLER, WIFE OF MEDAL OF HONOR RECIPIENT STAFF SGT. SALVATORE GIUNTA

"We take our families to war with us. Now, of course I don't mean that literally, but I mean it absolutely, figuratively, and I mean it emotionally."

GEN. MARTIN DEMPSEY

"It's hard work; it is great work though. It's rough. I don't want to sugarcoat it, but you can find something to love about this life. I always say, no matter what comes your way, in every challenge there's an opportunity to learn, and there's an opportunity to grow. Even on the bad days, I love what I do."

TARA CROOKS, ON BEING THE WIFE OF A SOLDIER

"Why? Why did you do it? What impelled you to put aside the instinct for self-preservation and risk your lives to take these cliffs? What inspired all the men of the armies that met here? We look at you, and somehow we know the answer. It was faith, and belief; it was loyalty and love."

RONALD REAGAN

"Working together, we cannot fail. Working together, we will prevail."

GEN. JOHN CAMPBELL

"Everything you need to be successful on this mission, you have. You have it up here [points to his head]. You have it in the guy standing next to you, and the guy standing behind you. That's ... what you've got."

LT. COL. SCOTT D. LEONARD

"You do what you've been trained to do. You do what your leaderships preach you to do. And you do what you know in your heart, and what you know up here is the right thing to do—on this mission specifically."

LT. COL. SCOTT D. LEONARD

"Every single man in this Army plays a vital role. Don't ever let up. Don't ever think that your job is unimportant. Every man has a job to do, and he must do it. Every man is a vital link in the great chain."

GEN. GEORGE PATTON

"Nothing you do in this regiment you have to do alone. There's somebody to help you through whatever it is that may be troubling you."

COL. JAMES BLACKBURN

"The Army has been my home. The Army has been my life. The Army has been my profession. The Army has been my love for all these many years. The Army has invested in me. It has taken chances on me. It has cared for me."

GEN. COLIN POWELL

"It is the people I'll remember. It was always about the people. It was about the soldiers who are well-trained but, at the end of the day, act out of faith in their leaders and each other; about the young sergeants who emerge from the ranks with strength, discipline, commitment, and courage."

GEN. STANLEY McCHRYSTAL

"You cannot be disciplined in great things and indiscipline in small things. Brave undisciplined men have no chance against the discipline and valor of other men. Have you ever seen a few policemen handle a crowd?"

GENERAL GEORGE S. PATTON JR.

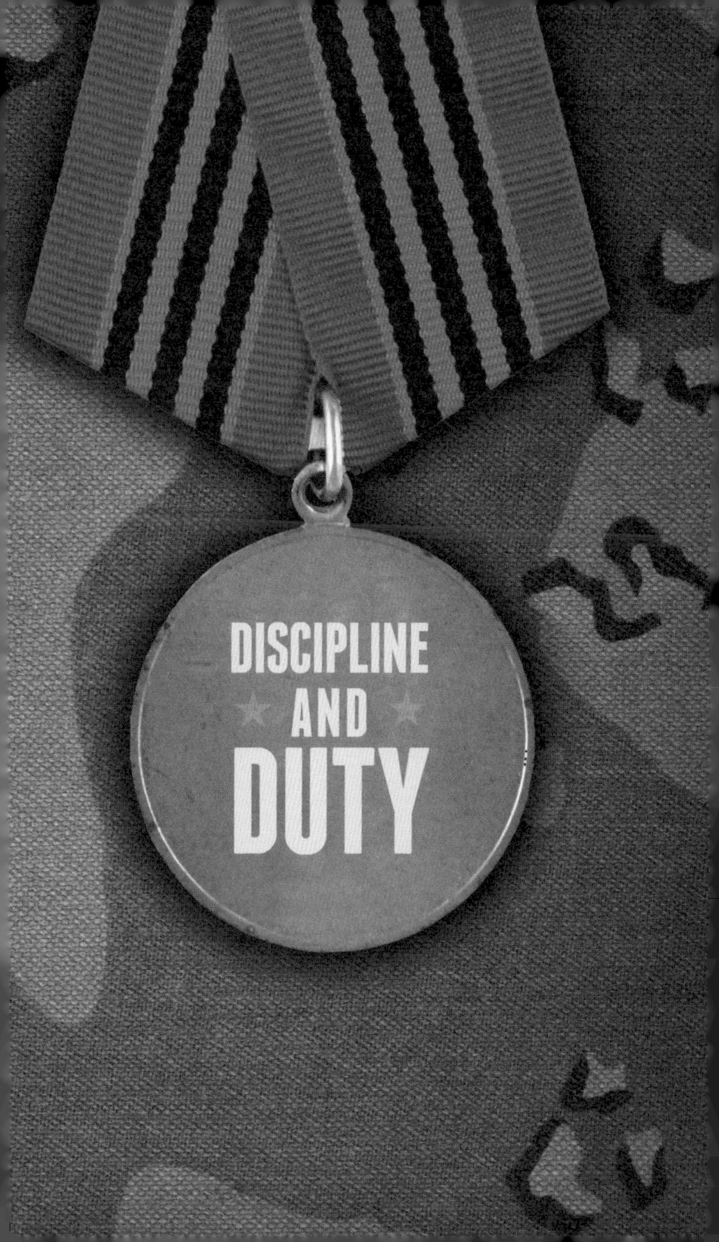
DISCIPLINE
AND
DUTY

★ ★ ★ ★ ★ ★ ★ ★ ★

"Absolute obedience to every command
is your first lesson. No matter what comes
you mustn't squeal. Think it over—all of you.
If any man wishes to withdraw
he will be gladly excused, for others are
ready to take his place."

TEDDY ROOSEVELT

Heroic Devotion

Near Cisterna di Littoria, Italy, Sergeant Sylvester Antolak charged 200 yards over flat, coverless terrain to destroy an enemy machine-gun nest during the second day of the offensive that broke through the German cordon of steel around the Anzio beachhead. Fully 30 yards in advance of his squad, he ran into withering enemy machine-gun, machine-pistol, and rifle fire. Three times he was struck by bullets and knocked to the ground, but each time he struggled to his feet to continue his relentless advance.

With one shoulder deeply gashed and his right arm shattered, he continued to rush directly into the enemy fire concentration with his submachine gun wedged under his uninjured arm until within 15 yards of the enemy strong point, where he opened fire at deadly close range, killing two Germans and forcing the remaining to surrender. He reorganized his men and, refusing to seek medical attention so badly needed, chose to lead the way toward another strong point 100 yards distant. Utterly disregarding the hail of bullets concentrated upon him, he had stormed ahead nearly three-fourths of the space between strong points when he was instantly killed by hostile enemy fire. But, inspired by Sergeant Antolak's courage, his squad went on to overwhelm the enemy troops.

By his supreme sacrifice, fighting courage, and heroic devotion to the attack, Sergeant Antolak was directly responsible for eliminating 20 Germans, capturing an enemy machine-gun, and clearing the path for his company to advance.

"Discipline is the soul of an army. It makes small numbers formidable; procures success to the weak, and esteem to all."

GEORGE WASHINGTON

"Most of the time, you're going, 'Why does this matter?' You know the fact that your socks are rolled a certain way don't matter. It's the fact that you pay attention to detail."

GEN. MARK WELSH III

"Whatever fatigues and sacrifices we may be called upon to undergo, let us have in view constantly the magnitude of the interests involved, and let each man determine to do his duty, leaving to an all-controlling Providence the decision of the contest."

GEN. GEORGE MEADE

"When you wear the uniform, you can't just change your mind because you get captured."

RETIRED COLONEL LEE ELLIS

"It's persistent. There's no 'let's go to the rear and take a break.' When you're in it, you're in it and it's part of your life. It's part of your daily life. It's a moment to moment."

GEN. MARTIN DEMPSEY

"Duty, Honor, Country— those three hallowed words reverently dictate what you ought to be, what you can be, what you will be. They are your rallying point to build courage when courage seems to fail, to regain faith when there seems to be little cause for faith, to create hope when hope becomes forlorn."

GEN. DOUGLAS MACARTHUR

"It is not my role to promise or prophesy.
Let it suffice to tell you, we know what we are
doing and what we want."

GEN. JOHN PERSHING

"Here in America we are descended in
blood and in spirit from revolutionaries
and rebels—men and women who dared
to dissent from accepted doctrine.
As their heirs, may we never confuse
honest dissent with disloyal subversion."

DWIGHT EISENHOWER

"Take your time. Stay away from the easy going.
Never take the same way twice."

GUNNERY SERGEANT CHARLES C. ARNDT

"The Constitution not only gives us freedoms,
but also entrusts us with certain responsibilities."

GEN. RICHARD MYERS

. . . .

"I discovered that nothing in life
is more liberating than to fight for
a cause that encompasses you but is not
defined by your existence alone.
And that has made all the difference, my
friends, all the difference in the world."

JOHN MCCAIN

. . . .

"The truth of the matter is that
you always know the right thing to do.
The hard part is doing it."

GEN. NORMAN SCHWARZKOFF

"I am a damned sight smarter man than Grant. I know more about military history, strategy, and grand tactics than he does. I know more about supply, administration, and everything else than he does. I'll tell you where he beats me though and where he beats the world. He doesn't give a damn about what the enemy does out of his sight, but it scares me like hell."

GEN. WILLIAM T. SHERMAN

"A young man who does not have what it takes
to perform military service is not likely
to have what it takes to make a living."

JOHN F. KENNEDY

"The burdens of military service
are borne disproportionately
by those who volunteer."

GEN. DAVID PETRAEUS

"But lest some unlucky event should happen
unfavorable to my reputation, I beg it may be
remembered by every gentleman in the room that
I this day declare with the utmost sincerity,
I do not think myself equal to the command
I am honored with."

GEORGE WASHINGTON

"We fight not to enslave, but to set a country free, and to make room upon the earth for honest men to live in."

THOMAS PAINE

"We must never forget that our democracy has survived because it was born in the crucible of public service."

LEON PANETTA

"At the end of the day what counts most are reputation and the ability to look in the mirror and know you made decisions based on mission and taking care of troopers and their families."

GEN. DAVID MCKIERNAN

"I like the fact that a couple of years ago an elected member of Congress felt compelled to publicly accuse the Marine Corps of being 'radical and extreme.' I like the fact that our Commandant informed that member of Congress that he was absolutely correct and that he passed on his thanks for the compliment."

COL. JAMES M. LOWE

"Whoever said the pen is mightier than the sword obviously never encountered automatic weapons."

GEN. DOUGLAS MACARTHUR

"I am not bound to win, but I am bound to be true. I am not bound to succeed, but I am bound to live by the light that I have. I must stand with anybody that stands right, stand with him while he is right, and part with him when he goes wrong."

ABRAHAM LINCOLN

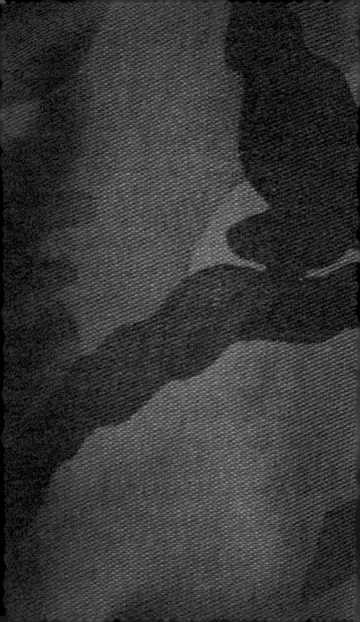

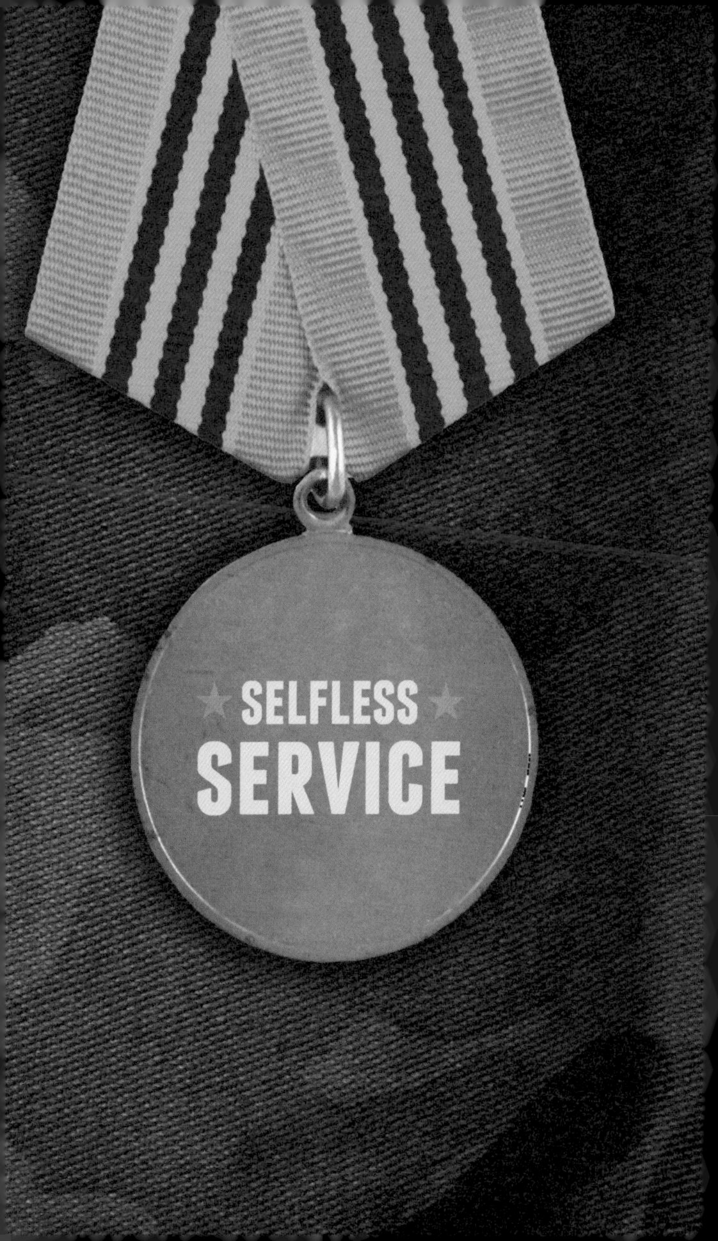
SELFLESS
SERVICE

"Every post is honorable in which
a man can serve his country."

GEORGE WASHINGTON

★ ★ ★ ★ ★ ★ ★ ★

HUMBLE HUMOR

"I was at a dinner party a couple of years ago when a woman approached and asked me what I did in the military. Not wishing to make a whole thing of it, I told her I work in the Pentagon. She kept pressing for details until I finally just admitted, not without a little pride, that I'm the joint chief's chairman. *Oh,* she said, her eyes suddenly downcast. *I guess I thought with all those medals and stars you were somebody important.*

But I am, I stressed. *I'm the President's top military adviser.* Her face turned ashen, her eyes got big. Clearly, she was embarrassed.

Oh my goodness, General Petraeus, I'm so sorry. I just didn't recognize you."

ADMIRAL MICHAEL MULLEN

"In the long history of the world, only a few generations have been granted the role of defending freedom in its hour of maximum danger. I do not shrink from this responsibility— I welcome it. I do not believe that any of us would exchange places with any other people or any other generation."

JOHN F. KENNEDY

"So here we are 33 years after I took the oath as a Second Lieutenant, and I have to tell you this is not exactly how I envisioned my life unfolding. Even as a young kid, all I ever wanted to do was teach Physical Education and raise a family. ... It was always clear to me that my Army experience was just going to be a two-year detour en route to my fitness profession."

GEN. ANN E. DUNWOODY
AT HER PROMOTION TO 4-STAR GENERAL

"I will thank God every day for the men and women in this country who are willing to put their lives on the line for all of us. They have responded to the call of the bugle with courage and with selfless dedication to country."

LEON PANETTA

FACT

The Lewis and Clark expedition was a military affair, with Captain Meriwether Lewis and Second Lieutenant William Clark leading a select group of volunteers.

"I am not influenced by the expectation of promotion or pecuniary reward. I wish to be useful, and every kind of service necessary for the public good, becomes honorable by being necessary."

NATHAN HALE

"And Classmates, we must remind our nation of the true definition and dynamic of homeland security. Protecting renewable energy is securing the homeland. Protecting the public from terrorists' strike is securing the homeland. Treating all people, whether migrant or felon, with human decency and mercy, is securing the home[land]. Saving lives is securing the homeland."

DeCarol Davis

"To all who will continue to serve after me, I ask only this, in parting: Make it matter."

Gen. Martin Dempsey

"I was silenced so quickly that I felt that possibly
I had suggested an unmilitary movement."

ULYSSES S. GRANT

. . . .

"They needed a sergeant;
and they jes' took me."

SGT. ALVIN YORK,
ON HOW HE CAME TO BE KNOWN AS "SERGEANT YORK"
WHEN HE WAS STILL TECHNICALLY ONLY A CORPORAL

. . . .

"How far I have succeeded in my endeavours (sic),
I submit to your Excellency's better judgment.
I hope I shall never be more fond of promotion
than studious to merit it. Modesty will ever
forbid me to apply to that House for any favors.
I consider myself immediately under your
Excellency's protection, and look up to you
for justice."

MAJ. GEN. NATHANAEL GREENE

WAAC

THIS IS MY WAR TOO!
WOMEN'S ARMY AUXILIARY CORPS
UNITED · STATES · ARMY

"And yet despite the repeated sacrifices,
they have answered the call to duty each time,
and stood in the gap between the evil that is
out there and our way of life."

LT. GEN. ROBERT L. CASLEN JR.

"While the Medal of Honor is awarded
to an individual, it is felt like anything
but an individual achievement.
It is ours—not mine."

STAFF SERGEANT RYAN PITTS

"I only regret that I have but one life
to lose for my country."

NATHAN HALE, BEFORE BEING HUNG BY THE BRITISH

"I'm no hero. Heroes are for the 'Late Show.'
I was just trying to help a couple of guys who
needed help."

SERGEANT PHILLIP ARTERBURY

"It has been the greatest of honors to have
soldiered with our nation's new greatest generation
in tough but important endeavors for the bulk
of that time. I can imagine no greater honor."

GEN. DAVID PETRAEUS

· · · · · · · · · · · · · · · **FACT** · · · · · · · · · · · · · · ·

While 32 of 44 U.S. presidents have served
in the military (either Armed Forces or militia),
Teddy Roosevelt is the only one who earned
the Medal of Honor.

"Your sons and daughters are among our nation's very best. They could have gone anywhere to college and had their choice of careers. Today they could be accepting a diploma and lucrative job offer instead of a commission in the United States Army. But they chose the path of Duty, Honor, and Country."

SECRETARY OF THE ARMY PETE GEREN

"It is impossible for the nation to compensate for the services of a fighting man. There is no pay scale that is high enough to buy the services of a single soldier even during a few minutes of the agony of combat, the physical miseries of the campaign."

GEN. GEORGE C. MARSHALL

★ ★ ★ ★ ★ ★ ★ ★

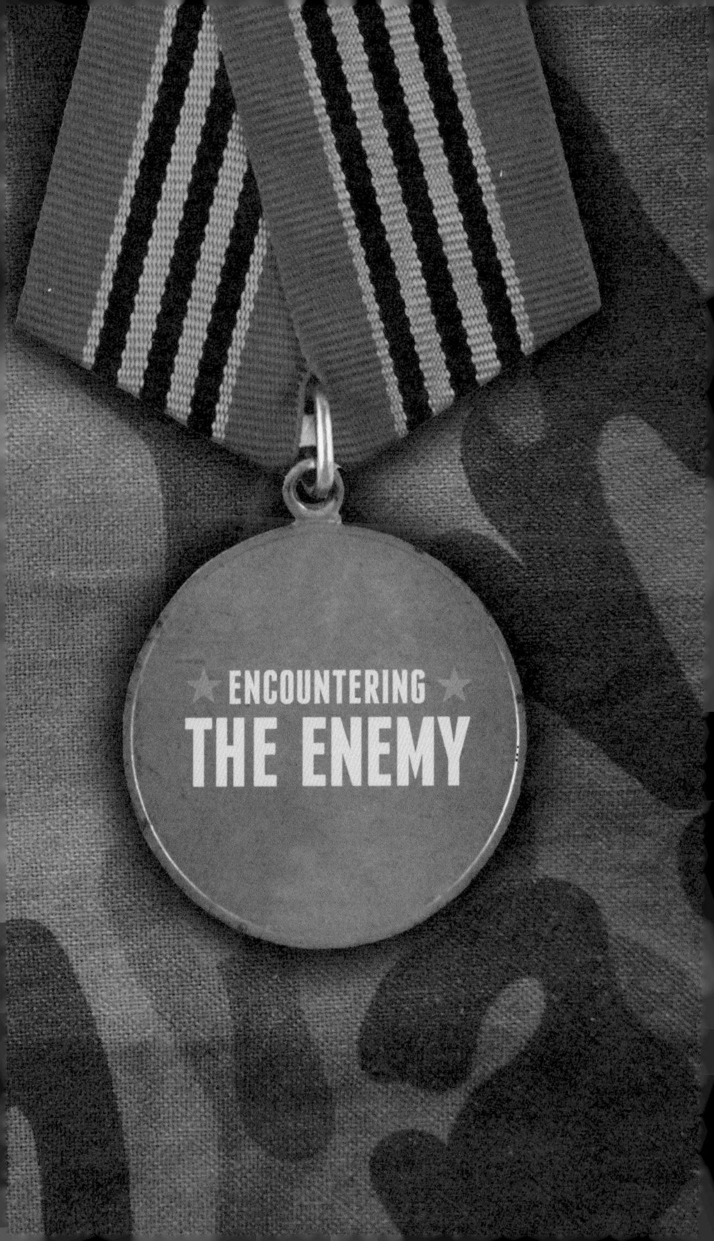
ENCOUNTERING
THE ENEMY

"Sighted sub, sank same."

LIEUTENANT DONALD F. MASON

★ ★ ★ ★ ★ ★ ★ ★ ★

'THIS MORNING WAS DIFFERENT'

"On October 3, 2009, Staff Sergeant Ty Carter awoke to a previously unseen volume of fire coming from the high ground surrounding the COP [combat outpost] ... occupied by the 53 men of Black Knight Troop. Only this morning was different, as an estimated 300 Taliban fighters fired recoilless rifles, rocket-propelled grenades, mortars, machine guns, and small arms at the COP.

Staff Sergeant Carter's responsibility that day was to support the guard positions, and in this capacity he twice sprinted through a barrage of fire to resupply ammunition and to fight alongside his desperately outnumbered comrades.

He moved into the open a third and fourth time to rescue a critically wounded teammate, render first aid, and carry him to safety. He again moved through withering fire to check on a fellow soldier and to secure a radio that later proved critical to saving the isolated team. He fought fearlessly and inspired those around him throughout that brutal day of combat."

GEN. JOHN F. CAMPBELL

"There is in combat a very singular focus.
You know exactly what you have to do.
Your purpose is defined, your mission is clear.
The enemy will always confuse you at times.
There'll be fog and friction, but you have a sense
of clarity that's uncanny in combat."

GEN. MARTIN DEMPSEY

"We have met the enemy,
and they are ours."

COMMODORE OLIVER HAZARD PERRY

"I realized the situation most keenly and felt
very uncomfortable. Lest there might be some
undue manifestation of this feeling on my
conduct, I said to myself, this is the duty
I undertook to perform for my country, and now
I'll do it, and leave the results with God."

LT. FREDERICK HITCHCOCK

"When the sword is once drawn,
the passions of men observe
no bounds of moderation."

ALEXANDER HAMILTON

"This war differs from other wars,
in this particular. We are not fighting
armies but a hostile people, and must
make old and young, rich and poor,
feel the hard hand of war."

GEN. WILLIAM TECUMSEH SHERMAN

"While a battle is raging one can see his
enemy mowed down by the thousand,
or the ten thousand, with great composure;
but after the battle these scenes are distressing,
and one is naturally disposed to do as much to
alleviate the suffering of an enemy as a friend."

ULYSSES S. GRANT

"If you find yourself in a fair fight,
you didn't plan your mission properly."

COL. DAVID HACKWORTH

"Early on in my career the fighter
saying was: 'Our mission is to fly
and fight and don't you ever forget it!'
After Vietnam we changed it to
'Our mission is to Fly, Fight and Win!'
We modernized, made training realistic
and professionalized the fighter force.
You saw the results in the First
Gulf War."

LT. GEN. ROBERT KELLEY, USAF (RET.)

"Our strategy in going after this army
is very simple. First we are going to cut it off,
and then we are going to kill it."

GEN. COLIN POWELL

"Suffice it to say, the close of the siege of Vicksburg found us with an army unsurpassed, in proportion to its numbers, taken as a whole of officers and men. A military education was acquired which no other school could have given."

ULYSSES S. GRANT

"Leadership is the art of getting someone else to do something you want done because he wants to do it."

DWIGHT EISENHOWER

· · · · · · · · · · · · · FACT · · · · · · · · · · · · ·

The term "gung ho" is a Chinese expression meaning "working together." It was adopted by Marine Lt. Col. Evans F. Carlson as the slogan of his Second Raider Battalion who followed him on the raid of Makin Island in 1942. The term soon spread throughout the U.S. Marine Corps as an expression of spirit and eventually entered the public dictionary to mean "enthusiastic" or "dedicated."

"This one guy said 'Surrender no die,
surrender no die, hands up, hands up.'
So, here I am facing about nine long guns
staring at me, and I decided that's probably
the best advice I was going to get that day,
so I went hands up."

RETIRED COLONEL LEE ELLIS

"I don't think I missed a shot.
It was no time to miss."

SGT. ALVIN YORK

"I was on Iwo Jima for 45 days.
I didn't get injured or anything,
and I owe it to three things: I prayed hard,
I dug deep, and I ran fast."

FORMER MARINE WILLIAM SCHOTT

★ ★ ★ ★ ★ ★ ★ ★

"If the enemy is in range, so are you."

INFANTRY JOURNAL

"Let it be known that if a farmer wishes to burn his cotton, his house, his family, and himself, he may do so. But not his corn. We want that."

GEN. WILLIAM TECUMSEH SHERMAN

"Gentlemen, if you do not batter us to pieces, we shall be starved out in a few days."

MAJOR ROBERT ANDERSON
AT THE BATTLE OF FORT SUMTER,
THE BEGINNING OF THE CIVIL WAR

"We're surrounded.
That simplifies the problem."

FIRST LIEUTENANT LEWIS B. "CHESTY" PULLER

"Retreat, hell! We're just attacking
in a different direction."

MARINE CORPS GEN. OLIVER P. SMITH

"I got hit with [a] piece of shrapnel.
It had gotten me inside the left leg.
I slid in a grazed out piece of ground.
The corpsman came. He took his forceps
and pulled it out and said, 'Do you want this?'
I said, 'I sure do!' It was still hot.
I still have it."

HERSHEL "WOODY" WILLIAMS, MEDAL OF HONOR RECIPIENT

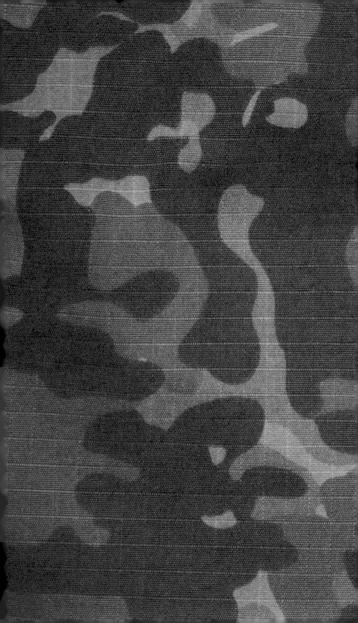

"It's nonlinear. It's everywhere.
There is no place to go to find sanctuary."

GEN. MARTIN DEMPSEY

★ ★ ★ ★ ★ ★ ★ ★

THE EXPLOITS OF WAR

"Many of the exploits of these men would fall under the head of romance; indeed, I am afraid that in telling some of their experiences, the romance got the better of the truth upon which the story was founded, and that, in the way many of these anecdotes are told, very little of the foundation is left. I suspect that most of them consist chiefly of the fiction added to make the stories better.

In one instance it was reported that a few men of [General William Tecumseh] Sherman's army passed a house where they discovered some chickens under the dwelling. They immediately proceeded to capture them, to add to the army's supplies. The lady of the house, who happened to be at home, made piteous appeals to have these spared, saying they were a few she had put away to save by permission of other parties who had preceded and who had taken all the others that she had.

The soldiers seemed moved at her appeal; but looking at the chickens again they were tempted and one of them replied: 'The rebellion must be suppressed if it takes the last chicken in the Confederacy,' and proceeded to appropriate the last one."

ULYSSES S. GRANT

"Nothing ruins a good war story
like an eyewitness."

GEN. STANLEY McCHRYSTAL

"Wars produce many stories of fiction,
some of which are told until they are
believed to be true."

ULYSSES S. GRANT

"We were sometimes amused by the music
of musket balls. One would come along with the
'meow' of a kitten, and the men would declare
the rebels were throwing kittens at them."

UNION SOLDIER S. F. FLEHARTY

"There is only one 'retirement plan' for terrorists."

MAJ. GEN. JAMES MATTIS

"Technology has advanced, new threats have emerged, and connections between people have increased exponentially. But through it all, the nature of conflict has remained constant."

GEN. RAYMOND ODIERNO

"Only a fool or a fraud sentimentalizes war."

JOHN MCCAIN

················· **FACT** ·················

The United States has sent its armed forces abroad more than 300 times "for other than normal peacetime purposes."
Officially, the country has only declared war on five occasions: the War of 1812, the Mexican-American War, the Spanish-American War, World War I, and World War II.

"Nothing is more depressing than to pass over ground where a battle has recently been fought. Any veteran will say that he prefers the advance to the retreat—the front to the rear of an army."

J.H. KIDD

"We shall cut no small figure through the country with our cannon."

HENRY KNOX,
CHIEF ARTILLERY OFFICER IN THE REVOLUTIONARY WAR
(LATER SECRETARY OF WAR)

"Gracious! What specimens of ghostliness they had left in there!"

OFFICER JOHN AMES

★ ★ ★ ★ ★ ★ ★ ★

"I hate war as only a soldier who has lived it can, only as one who has seen its brutality, its stupidity."

DWIGHT EISENHOWER

"War at all times, whether a civil war between sections of a common country or between nations, ought to be avoided, if possible with honor."

ULYSSES S. GRANT

"I know war as few other men now living know it, and nothing to me is more revolting. I have long advocated its complete abolition, as its very destructiveness on both friend and foe has rendered it useless as a means of settling international disputes."

GEN. DOUGLAS MACARTHUR

"Understand that the only thing worse
and more expensive than fighting and winning
a war is fighting and losing one."

GEN. MARK D. MILLEY

. . . .

"War's very object is victory,
not prolonged indecision.
In war there is no substitute
for victory."

GEN. DOUGLAS MACARTHUR

. . . .

"It was close; but that's the way it is in war.
You win or lose, live or die—
and the difference is just an eyelash."

GEN. DOUGLAS MACARTHUR

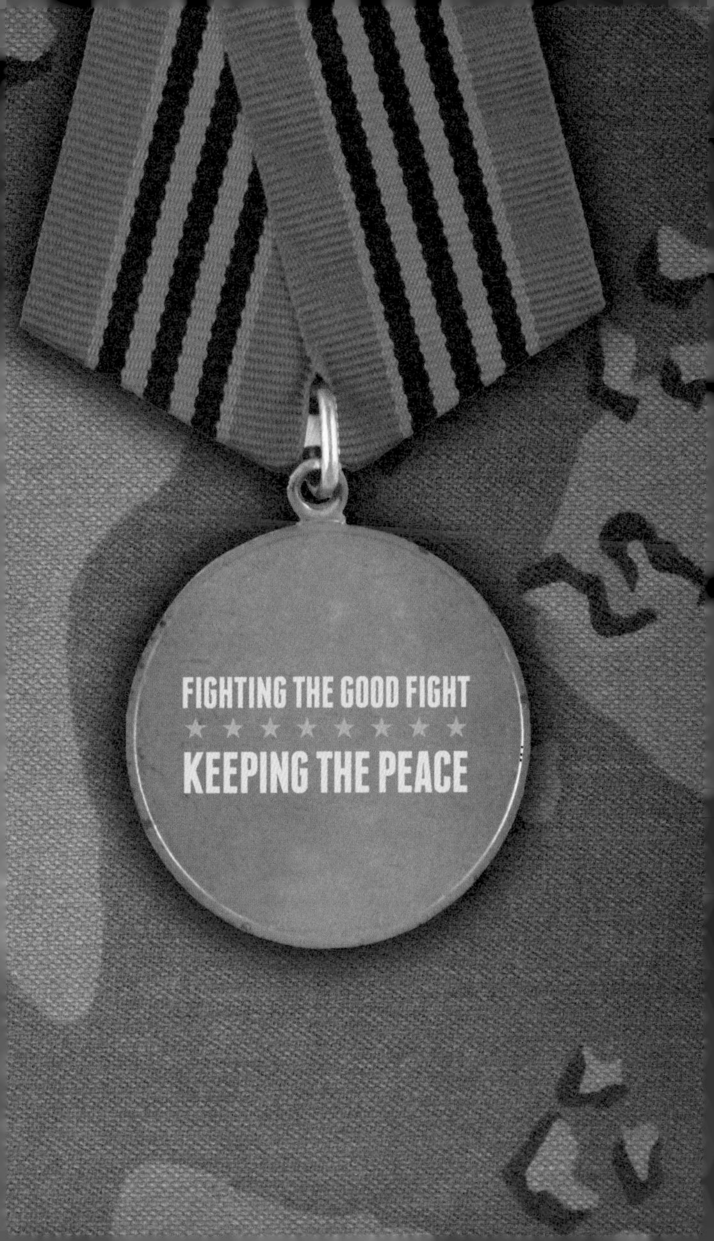
FIGHTING THE GOOD FIGHT
KEEPING THE PEACE

"Throughout our history, the fighting spirit of our fellow Americans has made clear that we never, never, never give up. Our forefathers, the pioneers, the immigrant families that came here all fought together to give our children that better life. We cannot fail to do the same."

LEON PANETTA

"Every man among us is more fit to meet the duties and responsibilities of citizenship because of the perils over which, in the past, the nation has triumphed; because of the blood and sweat and tears, the labor and the anguish, through which, in the days that have gone, our forefathers moved on to triumph."

TEDDY ROOSEVELT

★ ★ ★ ★ ★ ★ ★ ★

Moral Courage and Conviction

"Even at an early age, John Pershing demonstrated his moral courage and conviction. As a young school teacher during the late 1870s he taught local African-American students down the road in Prairie Mound, Missouri …which I may remind you, given the context of the times, was not a particularly popular or even socially accepted occupation. The negative stigma that may have been associated with his endeavors did not, however, deter John Pershing from what his upbringing had taught him to be the morally righteous path. As the story goes, one day a local bully barged into the schoolhouse and offered his… passionate opinion… that African-American children should not be afforded the opportunity to pursue an education. To which, John Pershing immediately confronted the man and forcibly removed him from the schoolhouse… Even at an early age… that was the kind of man John Pershing was… a man of conviction, moral decency, and courage. The ethical foundation instilled in him right here in central Missouri would continue to stay with him throughout his life and would have a fundamental impact on the exceedingly extraordinary man he was to become."

Lt. Gen. Robert L. Caslen

"They fought together as brothers in arms;
they died together and now they sleep side by side
. . . To them, we have a solemn obligation—
the obligation to ensure that their sacrifice
will help make this a better and safer world
in which to live."

ADMIRAL CHESTER NIMITZ

"To be prepared for war
is one of the most effectual means
of preserving peace."

GEORGE WASHINGTON

"In short, we are neither 'warmongers' nor
'appeasers,' neither 'hard' nor 'soft.'
We are Americans, determined to defend the
frontiers of freedom, by an honorable peace
if peace is possible, but by arms if arms
are used against us."

JOHN F. KENNEDY

"The men of Normandy had faith that what they were doing was right, faith that they fought for all humanity, faith that a just God would grant them mercy on this beachhead or on the next. It was the deep knowledge— and pray God we have not lost it— that there is a profound moral difference between the use of force for liberation and the use of force for conquest. You were here to liberate, not to conquer, and so you and those others did not doubt your cause. And you were right not to doubt."

RONALD REAGAN

"The hand of the aggressor is stayed
by strength—and strength alone."

DWIGHT EISENHOWER

"A house divided against
itself cannot stand."

ABRAHAM LINCOLN

"The soldier, above all other people,
prays for peace, for he must suffer and bear
the deepest wounds and scars of war."

GEN. DOUGLAS MACARTHUR

★ ★ ★ ★ ★ ★ ★ ★

"My life has been lived in the shadow of war—I almost lost my life in one. I hate war. I love peace. We have peace. And I am not going to let anyone take it away from us."

GEORGE H.W. BUSH

"Americans want a peaceful world. We know the terrible human and economic costs of past wars. We know that any future war may mean the end of all we value. Here again hunger is a primary menace. Wars are bred by poverty and oppression. Continued peace is possible only in a relatively free and prosperous world."

GEN. GEORGE C. MARSHALL

"Unjust war is to be abhorred; but woe to
the nation that does not make ready to hold its
own in time of need against all who would harm
it! And woe thrice over to the nation in which
the average man loses the fighting edge,
loses the power to serve as a soldier if the day
of need should arise!"

TEDDY ROOSEVELT

FACT

Teddy Roosevelt's exploits with the
"Rough Riders" during the Spanish-American
War are well-known. However, those
courageous exploits become all the more
impressive with the fact that Roosevelt resigned
his position as Assistant Secretary of the
Navy in order to serve in this unit.

"The eyes of the world are upon you.
The hopes and prayers of liberty-loving people
everywhere march with you."

DWIGHT D. EISENHOWER

....

"Let us exercise our responsibilities
as free people. But let us remember,
we are not enemies.
We are compatriots defending
ourselves from a real enemy."

JOHN MCCAIN

....

"Throughout the years our Army has kept
pace with a dynamic American society—
but always under civilian control. Our Armed
Forces are the staunchest supporters of our form
of government. They themselves would resist all
efforts to change that basic policy."

GEN. WILLIAM C. WESTMORELAND

"The fate of unborn millions will now depend, under God, on the courage and conduct of this army. Our cruel and unrelenting enemy leaves us only the choice of brave resistance, or the most abject submission. We have, therefore, to resolve to conquer or die."

GEORGE WASHINGTON

"To the Pacific basin has come the vista of a new emancipated world. Today, freedom is on the offensive, democracy is on the march. Today, in Asia as well as in Europe, unshackled peoples are tasting the full sweetness of liberty, the relief from fear."

GEN. DOUGLAS MACARTHUR

"Tyranny inevitably must retire before the tremendous moral strength of the gospel of freedom and self-respect for the individual, but we have to recognize that these democratic principles do not flourish on empty stomachs and that people turn to false promises of dictators because they are hopeless and anything promises something better than the miserable existence that they endure."

GEN. GEORGE C. MARSHALL

"I have lived my life and led my career with the abiding belief that when each of us who wear this uniform or choose to defend this nation are called, we will do the right thing."

GEN. PAUL SELVA

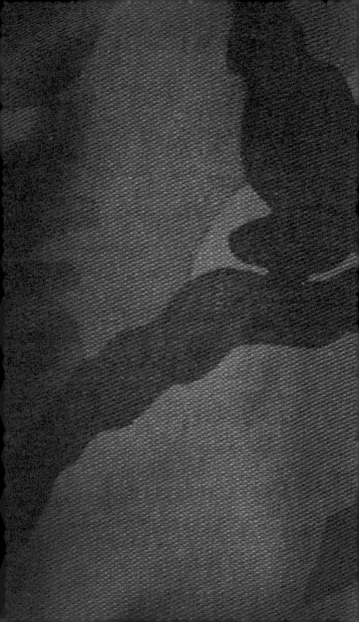

UNCOMMON CHARACTER

★ ★ ★ ★ ★ ★ ★

EXEMPLARY SPIRIT

"I am determined to defend my rights
and maintain my freedom or
sell my life in the attempt."

MAJ. GEN. NATHANAEL GREENE

★ ★ ★ ★ ★ ★ ★ ★ ★

True Grit

"On April 10 [2001], two months into the deployment, [Staff Sergeant Travis Mills'] world changed forever. While on a patrol, an IED [improvised explosive device] tore through his frame, and he sustained life-threatening injuries. One week later, he arrived at Walter Reed National Military Medical Center. Remarkably, after just a few weeks, he was in outpatient care working on his rehabilitation.

Staff Sergeant Mills is one of only five quadruple amputees in the military to ever survive the severity of losing four limbs, but even that challenge has done nothing to slow him down. He does physical and occupational therapy for almost nine hours a day, and his trainers tell us he is always the last one to leave the building. Six weeks after his injury, he took his first steps, and he has been relearning to walk on his new legs alongside his now-walking baby daughter, one-year-old Chloe. . . . His perseverance and his strength—that is what our Army is all about. So when you are feeling sorry for yourself, I want you to think about Staff Sergeant Mills."

Gen. Raymond Odierno

"The U.S. military is composed of many parts: exceptional ships, planes and ground systems, unparalleled institutions and infrastructure, the finest of high technology and world-class networks that enable all that we do. But as all here appreciate, I know, the essence, the core of our military is and always will be its people: men and women who raise their right hands and recite the oath of enlistment."

GEN. DAVID PETRAEUS

"The men and women of your Armed Forces are the best we've ever known. They believe in what they are doing. And all I ask is that you continue to believe in them."

ADMIRAL MICHAEL MULLEN

"The history of free men is never really written by chance—but by choice—their choice."

DWIGHT EISENHOWER

"They go into harm's way to protect us and to provide for the common defense. They are the best and the very brightest of America's youth, and the greatest of all honors I have had was the honor of being one of them and of being their senior representative over the past four years."

GEN. COLIN POWELL

"There is no higher calling, no more honorable choice than the one that you here today have made. To join the Armed Forces is to be prepared to make the ultimate sacrifice for your country and for your fellow man."

GEORGE H.W. BUSH

"Among the Americans serving on Iwo Island, uncommon valor was a common virtue."

ADMIRAL CHESTER NIMITZ

"I have just left your fighting sons in Korea. They have met all tests there, and I can report to you without reservation that they are splendid in every way."

GEN. DOUGLAS MACARTHUR

"Wars may be fought with weapons, but they are won by men. It is the spirit of the men who follow and of the man who leads that gains the victory."

GEN. GEORGE PATTON

★ ★ ★ ★ ★ ★ ★ ★

"Since coming to the Army, it has dawned on me that it is [Arlington National Cemetery], not the Mall's monuments and memorials, that tells the story of our great nation."

SECRETARY OF THE ARMY PETE GEREN

"It is foolish and wrong to mourn the men who died. Rather we should thank God that such men lived."

GEN. GEORGE PATTON

"Their devotion has seen our country through its darkest hours and ensured that the light of freedom continues to shine over our land. It is a debt of honor and service that can never be repaid."

GEN. DAVID MCKIERNAN

"I pay supreme tribute to our officers and soldiers of the line. When I think of their heroism, their patience under hardships, their unflinching spirit of offensive action, I am filled with emotions which I am unable to express. Their deeds are immortal and they have earned the eternal gratitude of our country."

GEN. JOHN PERSHING

"Ask not what your country can do for you— ask what you can do for your country."

JOHN F. KENNEDY

"Live for something rather than die for nothing."

GEN. DOUGLAS MACARTHUR

"Under all those disadvantages no men ever show more spirit or prudence than ours. In my opinion, nothing but virtue has kept our army together through this campaign."

COLONEL JOHN BROOKS

"Military power wins battles, but spiritual power wins wars."

GEN. GEORGE C. MARSHALL

"I'm honored by your presence, and mindful that I speak to an audience that can discern truth from falsehood in a politician's appraisal of the war. You know, better than most, whether our cause is just, necessary, and winnable. You have risked much to make it so. Thank you."

JOHN McCAIN

★ ★ ★ ★ ★ ★ ★ ★

"The Navy and Marine Corps are
America's away team.
We don't get any home games.
We're not just in the right place
at the right time,
we're in the right place all the time.
We get on station faster,
we stay there longer,
we bring everything we need with us."

SECRETARY RAY MABUS

"I have a good deal of say over what happens
in the Navy, but when the time comes to take
the fight to the enemy, it's not me sitting in
the hot seat … it's that Sailor, Marine,
Coastguardsman, Soldier, and Airman …
and I am keenly aware of that fact."

SECRETARY GORDON R. ENGLAND

"I hope I shall possess firmness and virtue enough to maintain what I consider the most enviable of all titles, the character of an honest man."

George Washington

"I felt like anything rather than rejoicing at the downfall of a foe who had fought so long and valiantly, and had suffered so much for a cause, though that cause was, I believe, one of the worst for which a people ever fought, and one for which there was the least excuse."

Ulysses S. Grant

"No organization can excel for very long without a culture of integrity."

Admiral James A. Winnefeld

"I am certain that after the dust of centuries has passed over our cities, we, too, will be remembered not for victories or defeats in battle or in politics, but for our contribution to the human spirit."

JOHN F. KENNEDY

"You have belonged, then, to the greatest army, the most splendid army of modern times, under probably the best organization and composed of a personnel unequaled in modern times with an aggressiveness and fighting spirit unsurpassed by any."

GEN. JOHN PERSHING

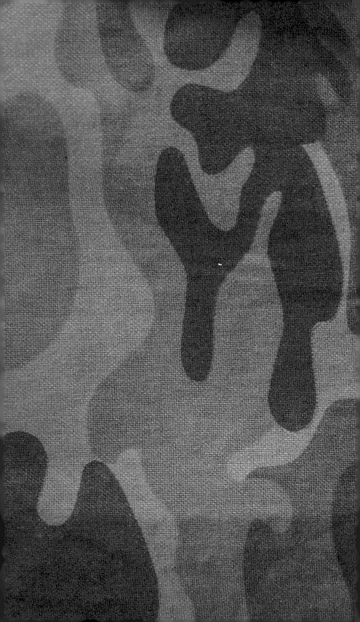

DARE
★ TO BE ★
GREAT

"We must dare to be great; and we must realize that greatness is the fruit of toil and sacrifice and high courage. …We are face to face with our destiny and we must meet it with a high and resolute courage. For us is the life of action, of strenuous performance of duty; let us live in the harness, striving mightily; let us rather run the risk of wearing out than rusting out."

TEDDY ROOSEVELT

THE SKY'S THE LIMIT

"I knew two things when I graduated from high school. Two, that's all I knew. And they were both negative. Under no circumstances was I going to go into the Marine Corps. I lived in … Columbia, South Carolina, an hour and a half drive from Parris Island. On the weekend, Marines came into town because back then, you know, where else were the black Marines going to go? But they'd come to Columbia and they'd go to Drew Park swimming pool where I worked, and I got to see Marines up close and personal. They were crazy. And then I did not want to fly airplanes. I thought that was inherently dangerous. So the two things I knew was I would not fly, and I would not be a Marine.

My very first year at the Marine Corps, I mean at the Naval Academy, my first company officer was a gentleman by the name of Major John Riley Love who was an infantry officer, so much like my dad. He was tough, but incredibly fair. And although we were together for just one year for my freshmen year at the Naval Academy, he so impressed me that my senior year I said, 'I want to be like him.'"

CHARLES BOLDEN, HEAD OF NASA

"And any man who may be asked in this century what he did to make his life worthwhile, I think can respond with a good deal of pride and satisfaction: 'I served in the United States Navy.'"

JOHN F. KENNEDY

"A recent survey about why people join the military found that the number one reason was pride, self-esteem, and honor, followed by a desire to better their lives, and then duty and obligation to country, and then everything else you would imagine came after that. Now, I would sure want to hire someone mature enough at a young age to think of country before self."

ADMIRAL JAMES A. WINNEFELD

"Those years that I was in the Navy became some of the most consequential years of my life. It taught me responsibility, taught me the importance of making a decision. It taught me the importance of doing something bigger than myself and how you had to be part of a bigger structure."

SECRETARY OF THE NAVY RAY MABUS

"One of West Point's great lessons—if, or when we recognize it, is that we don't accomplish anything by ourselves."

GEN. MARTIN DEMPSEY

"If my life had shared no common purpose, it would not have amounted to much more than eccentricity. There is no honor or happiness in just being strong enough to be left alone."

JOHN MCCAIN

West Point's Class of 2005 is known as
the "Class of 9/11," as the attacks occurred
during their freshman year. By coincidence,
there were 911 graduates in this class.

"We must ensure that we remain Number One. We cannot do it by just saying it. We must remain Number One and face the challenges of not only today but also tomorrow."

GEN. MARK D. MILLEY

"Whatever path you choose, be excellent and don't settle for mediocrity. If you strive to be the best, nobody can question you or your capabilities."

CAPT. KATIE HIGGINS

"I worked hard. I belonged to an institution that was only concerned about your performance and your potential. The army, in those days, was the most socially progressive institution for blacks in this country while segregation was still the law of the land in so many parts of our country. It worked for me mostly because I loved doing something that was dear to my heart and that was being a soldier."

GEN. COLIN POWELL

"The military will not be able to train or educate you to have all the right answers—as you might find in a manual—but you should look for those experiences and pursuits in your career that will help you at least ask the right questions."

ROBERT GATES

"You have received a strengthening of character, you have received a breadth of vision which you had not before and you have prepared yourselves, unconsciously, to take up the duties that will devolve upon you when you return to your homes and to your firesides."

GEN. JOHN PERSHING

"The Army is an easy business. You will get from it what you put into it."

1ST SGT. SANDREA CRUZ

"Each one of us is responsible for maintaining the highest standards of character, competence, and resiliency in ourselves, our families, and our soldiers. Mentorship of soldiers is critical so that leaders help soldiers grow from their experiences and deal with periods of personal adversity within an environment of mutual trust."

GEN. RAYMOND ODIERNO

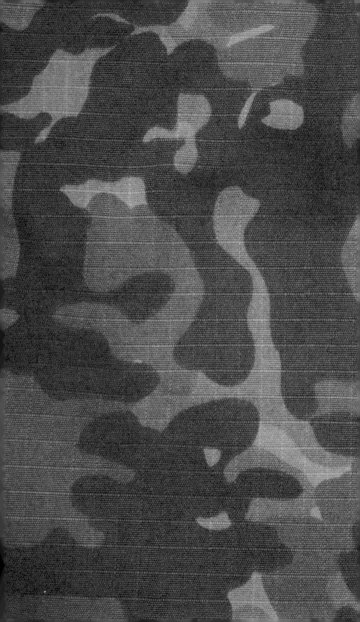

LESSONS
FOR LIFE
★ ★ ★ ★ ★ ★ ★
AND FUTURE LEADERS

"A competent leader can get efficient service from poor troops, while on the contrary an incapable leader can demoralize the best of troops."

GEN. JOHN PERSHING

"Leadership is a gift.
It's given by those who follow,
but you have to be worthy of it."

GEN. MARK WELSH III

"The essence of leadership is to get others to do something because they think you want it done and because they know it is worthwhile doing."

DWIGHT EISENHOWER

BEYOND THE CALL OF DUTY

Commander Richard Nott Antrim went well beyond the call of duty while interned as a prisoner of war of the enemy Japanese in the city of Makassar, Celebes, Netherlands East Indies, in April 1942.

Acting instantly on behalf of a naval officer who was subjected to a vicious clubbing by a frenzied Japanese guard venting his insane wrath upon the helpless prisoner, Comdr. (then Lt.) Antrim boldly intervened, attempting to quiet the guard and finally persuading him to discuss the charges against the officer. With the entire Japanese force assembled and making extraordinary preparations for the threatened beating, and with the tension heightened by 2,700 Allied prisoners rapidly closing in, Comdr. Antrim courageously appealed to the fanatic enemy, risking his own life in a desperate effort to mitigate the punishment.

When the other had been beaten unconscious by 15 blows of a hawser and was repeatedly kicked by three soldiers to a point beyond which he could not survive, Comdr. Antrim gallantly stepped forward and indicated to the perplexed guards that he would take the remainder of the punishment, throwing the Japanese completely off balance in their amazement and eliciting a roar of acclaim from the suddenly inspired Allied prisoners. By his fearless leadership and valiant concern for the welfare of another, he not only saved the life of a fellow officer and stunned the Japanese into sparing his own life but also brought about a new respect for American officers and men, and a great improvement in camp living conditions.

"I can say, with great truth, that ever since I had the honor to serve under you, I have been more attentive to the public interest, and more engaged in the support of your Excellency's character, than ever I was to my own ease, interest, or reputation."

MAJ. GEN. NATHANAEL GREENE,
LETTER TO GEORGE WASHINGTON

"Caution and cynicism are safe, but soldiers don't want to follow cautious cynics. They follow leaders who believe enough to risk failure or disappointment for a worthy cause."

GEN. STANLEY MCCHRYSTAL

"Dependability, integrity, the characteristic of never knowingly doing anything wrong, that you would never cheat anyone, that you would give everybody a fair deal. Character is a sort of an all-inclusive thing. If a man has character, everyone has confidence in him. Soldiers must have confidence in their leader."

GEN. OMAR BRADLEY

"All lives are a struggle against selfishness."

JOHN MCCAIN

"Make sure you give a good measure of your time and your talent and your treasure in service to others. The need to serve others has never been greater in our nation. Money and position will or will not follow but satisfaction will always be there. Always have a purpose in life that is beyond position and money."

GEN. COLIN POWELL

"Plans are worthless, but planning is everything."

DWIGHT EISENHOWER

"It is time that we steered by the stars, not by the lights of each passing ship."

GEN. OMAR BRADLEY

"Army: A body of men assembled to rectify the mistakes of the diplomats."

SECRETARY OF THE NAVY JOSEPHUS DANIELS

"No man can be a great officer who is not infinitely patient of details, for an army is an aggregation of details."

GEORGE STILLMAN HILLARD

"Go back to your command, and try to think what we are going to do ourselves, instead of what Lee is going to do."

ULYSSES S. GRANT

"If human beings were pawns it would be different, but they are our own men."

GEN. JOHN PERSHING

"The Chinese use two brush strokes to write the word 'crisis.' One brush stroke stands for danger; the other for opportunity. In a crisis, be aware of the danger—but recognize the opportunity."

JOHN F. KENNEDY

· · · · · · · · · · · · · · · **FACT** · · · · · · · · · · · · · ·

Legendary Confederate General Robert E. Lee was offered—and turned down—a top command in the Union Army during the Civil War.

· ·

"I'm constantly reminded that incredibly bright adults will work extremely long hours perfecting fundamentally flawed concepts."

ADMIRAL JAMES A. WINNEFELD

"If we should have to fight, we should be prepared to do battle from the neck up instead of from the neck down."

GEN. JIMMY DOOLITTLE

"If we continue to develop our technology without wisdom or prudence, our servant may prove to be our executioner."

GEN. OMAR BRADLEY

"You know as well as I do that counterinsurgency is a very nuanced type of military operation."

GEN. JOHN ABIZAID

"No commander was ever privileged to lead a finer force; no commander ever derived greater inspiration from the performance of his troops."

GEN. JOHN PERSHING

· ·

"Second lieutenant bars weigh only a few ounces, but the weight of what they represent is profound."

GEN. MARTIN DEMPSEY

· ·

"The officer is the keystone of the military arch. No army can carry out a difficult task; indeed it can scarcely perform the routine functions of peace without an efficient officer corps."

DWIGHT D. EISENHOWER

★ ★ ★ ★ ★ ★ ★ ★ ★

"We are a microcosm of our society—
where all our country's races, religions,
and creeds—equally share in the task of defending
our Nation and its Constitution. Consequently,
our military's character and ethic is a reflection
of your own."

Lt. Gen. Robert L. Caslen Jr.

"History does not repeat,
but it does rhyme."

Gen. Martin Dempsey

"If I've learned nothing else in forty years it's that,
no matter how smart you think you are—
you can't read people's minds and you can't
predict the future—so change is the norm."

Gen. George W. Casey Jr.

"We few, we happy few, we band of brothers;
For he to-day that sheds his blood with me
Shall be my brother…"

SHAKESPEARE'S *HENRY V*

★ ★ ★

DID YOU ENJOY THIS BOOK
OR HAS IT TOUCHED YOUR LIFE IN SOME WAY?
WE'D LOVE TO HEAR FROM YOU!

PLEASE SEND YOUR COMMENTS TO:
HALLMARK BOOK FEEDBACK
P.O. BOX 419034
MAIL BOX 100
KANSAS CITY, MO 64141

OR E-MAIL US AT:
BOOKNOTES@HALLMARK.COM